Ideas for Human Evolution

Education

There are many different forms of education all throughout the world but I think it should be mentioned that there is a desperate demand for new models of education. Within most democratic nations or educated societies, I think it can be argued that there is a steep decline in individual wellness due to the increased usage of coping strategies and anxiety. Certainly there are numerous factors beyond education that play a role in this, but I think it should be noted that our standard model of education is obsolete. The level of bullying and judgment that goes on inside of schools as well as academic pressure does not have to exist. I realize there are going to be private schools to help disclose how public schools can operate but even private schools may very well have big flaws within that system.

One of the biggest flaws that takes place is the treatment of individuals, especially children as if they don' t know anything. It is to my knowledge that children and young people that may not be "sufficiently educated" have built-in knowledge about how life works. I call it the intuitive spirit that dwells often in greater measure in younger aged individuals than older individuals because the current system is designed to suggest that one person in the room knows it all and others don' t. Many people will argue that children and young people cannot survive in this world without standard levels of education and they are correct, but what these people and experts don't realize are a number of things.

It is becoming more obvious in this current age that not everyone learns in the same way, as we now have concepts of people who are auditory and visually prone to learn versus from just shoving down information. We may have a variety of subjects in which there are a multitude of fields in daily life whereby a demand for life needs supplying, but many of these fields are stagnating and degrading because there isn't much openness for reform purely based on strict material analytics where proof is unanimously approved by the academic establishment. In other words, many of our systems today operate from a purely materialistic POV that excludes new industries and fields that could make older systems obsolete.

Not everyone is going to need to know a whole lot about science, mathematics, literature, and history. Certainly there are basics that everyone can agree is helpful at different times in our life, but if you ask the average person how much they remember from their elementary and or perhaps there undergrad studies, there will be a significant void in their ability to remember exactly because the information wasn't critical to their soul or psyche. Psyche means soul in Greek and it's important that

we realize that we all have different capabilities
meant to be explored without aggressive pressure.

But one of the last points about education is
the way the teacher interacts, specifically if they are
coming from a place where they think they know
everything and can't learn from the youngest in
front of them everyday. Teachers should treat
students like equals and just because they may not
have the memorized structure of the world paradigm,
it's important we teach in ways that respects the
desire and need for a new paradigm that can't be
fostered in without loosening the ends from what we
think is critical information. Certainly we give people
degrees for being able to discern what is critical
information and applying that, but if standard
education can't even acknowledge the emergency of
widespread exploitative and financial inequality, this
institution is also responsible for the suffering of
humanity.

Science

We all know science in its core is a process of investigation versus an ideological institution but in large part the reverse has controlled the narrative. A certain divide of knowledge which we can say is scientifically based has crept its way into the collective mindset and that is the idea that science and very technical experiments cannot be understood by most people. Science or rather a certain group of people that has used the name of science, have gone into the extreme mindset of creating investigations on how the world works while ignoring or manipulating evidence to suggest there is evidence to prove a contrary opinion. This group of people can often be termed as intellectual materialists that sprung up quite evidently after the European enlightenment. By using many of the horrible events and beliefs that institutional religion placed upon society, an unspoken initiative has been waged upon the battlefield of academia to blot out the authority of not just religion but of any evidence suggesting other forms and forces of intelligence working in the universe.

There have certainly been a number of quacks, charlatans, and spiritual cults led by false gurus that have affected the credibility of this other field of knowledge. On the other hand, there have also been a number of credible scientists that have been able to score a critical percentage of the public's interest with some insider validation amongst academia to keep the movement for another source of reliable knowledge alive. Much of the information suggests the human conscience has a direct effect on the material universe and that there could be many alternative ways to not just treat human illness but to deliver high quantities of environmentally friendly energy without depending on fossil fuels, nuclear plants, and renewable energy.

Humanity is reaching a point of critical mass where certain public information will hit a capacity of overload causing many of the sources of storage for public information to either reset or reconfigure its mainframe. Through the scientific institution that has highly altered the way academia configures reliable knowledge, a huge overlay of extreme polarization has affected the way humanity can solve or even transcend various types of mass suffering. The current mindset of science is so materialistic bent on breaking the universe into smaller and smaller pieces to attain valid proof that a whole array of reliable knowledge for evolving human life is becoming less and less of a focus for human renovation.

Right now science requires a massive transition to a new approach for what we really want to aim for and right now science obviously cares very little about the increase in poverty while ignoring the science on not just economic inequality but on how energy is a spectrum of consciousness that is built into parallel universes that thereby creates a material universe. Many more things can be said about science and some of the great advancements we have come to recognize, but from survival of the fittest, to natural selection, to the big bang, there are many things that science has tried to explain with objective analysis but really have no basis in reality. For how could a random event with a finite quantity of energy that we call the big bang create a universe where order and consecutive expansion upon that order exist, a random event that could create biological and intelligent life? The denial of consciousness is the utmost priority through most of the academic investigations that to this day show disinterest in funding investigators to extrapolate and perhaps prove something revolutionary.

Religion

Another source for many human beings for reliable knowledge is said to come from religion and yet there have been countless atrocities created from the very hierarchs who have claimed to be the leader or a particular faith. On the contrary, if we look to many of the arbiters who brought in what many might call religion but really was a system of consciousness, there was very little evidence to prove that these arbiters wanted to inculcate the masses through fear, violence, and theocratic tyranny. There are many scholars who are historians or theologians and claim to understand many of the ancient texts, some of the manipulations that happened upon those texts, and the overall trend to create a religion. But what many scholars don't realize is that much of the information from the arbiters was actually erased and twisted but even more so manipulated from the point of strategic idolization.

Religion is in its last days although it's not to say that some of the ideas built into religion or what is really mysticism will be held in various proportions to support various social industries, some of which have yet to surface. There may be a lot of people who support religion around the world but many of these people are experiencing a growing resistance and objectionable challenge to accepting themselves without shame and choosing to live life differently. Religion is like a coat of mud or tar that often drags the lives of many into a very narrowly descriptive or expressive outlet. People are needing different outlets, new ways to find and express themselves than ever before because current systems or ideas are often only reinforcing entropy or suffering though the experts will always blame some other scapegoat that is really insignificant to the current state of affairs.

In some sense, religion is meant to be a morale booster for the masses and in another sense it's meant to help people challenge elitism but the fact of the matter remains to be seen where these two directives have been met. There will be people over time who are going to try to help religion get back into its mystical roots but only time will tell if they will be able to be successful. The biggest lie that has been created from religion which I won't blame the founding arbiters for because elitism or tyranny has its origins from the beginning of recorded history, but the idea that this thing called god is separated from human beings and that humans are not god in the sense that the universe is an interconnected whole whereby we the creations of the creator could be disconnected or of lower value than the source is narcissistic in truth.

Religion will be facing many difficulties over the years and it will remain to be seen as a positive institution to help lead people unto a path of mastery, a path of enlightenment unless it questions itself. Any intuition that doesn't question itself or rather have debates and seeks to bring attention to controversies and taboos will undergo a path of thermodynamics. Alongside the abuse through the name of god, the other abuse that will need confronting is the idolatry branded upon many of the arbiters who never really wanted credit or praise for what they experienced was a universal force that is built into everyone and everything. But certain hegemonies knew how to leverage an idolatrous social paradigm to interlock any form of resistance or uprising that could be revolutionary, non-violent, and anti-elitist. Religion may be in its end days but they say that the end is just the beginning to new human relationships for how we see this whole simulation as a positive force.

Agriculture

Right now most agriculture is corporatized meaning that the rules in which mass cultivation of food products is organized is centralized often with the incentive to gain quick profits and to restrict holistic measures. One of the main issues in modern day agriculture is the tilling of the soil which erodes the nutrition that gives plants high quantities of life force or performance. Life force is not always traceable through the study of which nutrients in quantification there is upon the plant biology. Life force is a component that deals with the quality of the energy that plants use to grow. There is very little investigation into this field of knowledge because it would compromise quick and easy methods to gain quick profit and keep the majority of employees and customers from reaping the full benefits of a holistic system.

There are various systems out there that prove you can farm without tilling the soil but the investigative studies on how this can be done is yet to be funded or opened for professional establishment acceptance. Biodynamic, permaculture, hydroponic, aquaponic, and various models of "no till" methods do exist creating an agricultural high quality effect of nutritional life force. This topic seems like a pseudo-scientific claim but various practices around the world that deal with traditional medicine from India to China have proven there is another element to the function of life not just in people but ecology.

As climate change begins to increase in power and as economic currencies become more unstable, the agricultural domain will remain unstable if it is a field of commerce highly dependent on imports than exports. It will be important for nations and local communities to begin growing their food which will require more financial independence given to citizens to have time to participate in integral life practices versus oftentimes being exploited many times over through another corporation or business. The dependency on corporations with a centralized hierarchy will become less and less trustworthy to operate as problems increase in size and power causing people to protest for the regulation of not just wealth inequality but business ownership models to thereby give people a vote in how a business is run.

New industries will arise causing a change in how people eat and relate to the food they eat as the current paradigm holds a very autocratic relationship for how to prepare and consume food. There are many people in the food industry who have very little appreciation for themselves which affects many of the ways food is processed and delivered to people. As arbitrary as this may sound without specific citations, new technologies will arise to determine

which foods people will need given their body type.
Right now there is a huge detriment to having
agriculture mass mechanized whereby the dependency
on machines versus people to do the work is
significantly misappropriating holistic systems to the
dustbin. Certain technologies or machines are
important but to almost completely designate the
industry to as few workers as possible incentives the
work and product quality to the lowest common
denominator.

A greater life purpose will come into the lives
of community members who are given the knowledge
about alternatives to our mass corporatised models of
farming which will inspire people to involve
themselves through an ethic that will create new
positive relationships with others but also with the
earth from which we are given life. Without this
relationship, human beings are bound to increase in
suffering through the fallout of this vital industry
that fulfills various needs that aren' t just survival
based but also in relating to oneself.

Politics

Often termed as a game of power, I might call it false power even though it seems relatively realistic in terms of authority to control people. True power in my opinion is a state of mind versus a position or status of authority. To be more clear of what this state of mind is, it incorporates values of unconditional love, fearlessness, and universal synergy, knowing that the actions and ideas we project onto others will be reciprocated back unto us. I realize politics is very boring to many people because it deals with a pool of information that is often leveraged by aristocratic classes and systems, but in certain ways it still affects the current state to a certain degree that is overrated. I do believe journalism, activism, media coverage, and various organizational structures to educate and reform society is important, but we must not forget there is a source of reliable knowledge that is often outside party politics which often doesn' t ascribe to a specific party.

This source of knowledge is integral for helping the public build a sincere base of reliable knowledge and it in some fashion was a form of philosophy but this form has died out and a new industry is waiting to arise that has not yet come. Academia has a lot of work to get its act together and the field of unified physics and mysticism are integral for assisting the great wall of intellectualism that has waged war upon the hearts and souls of people. There have been few to comment that virtually everything in society can be discussed in a political light but certainly people can take this into extremes. Right now party politics is denying or ignoring a pretty big hole in the ceiling that relates to the redistribution of wealth but on the other hand politics gets so focused on the semantics, the numbers in a sort of perfectionist light, that it often ignores the voices of the unheard.

There are many laws that could get passed right away from the system of checks and balances which is a very operable and well designed system, but further between partisan rhetoric it does not have to matter so much if the people will organize common ground and demonstrate. The level of inspiration for people to actually do this is another thing, but a certain level of demonstration can be a very scary thing for people in power because it has the capacity to threaten their comfortable luxurious position if they do not comply. But even the idea of having a wealthy lifestyle from being a political leader is growing more and more suspicious in post capitalist materialism whereby new standards of luxury might be reset.

Politics is going through a very slow new birth at the moment and that is because of the radical suppression of various pools of reliable knowledge in academia, but it can be seen in the foreseeable future that a new system of politics is created with technology whereby long-time spans from which officials are elected can be shortened by the vote of the people. A system of direct democracy is a very possible reality in the near future whereby the people can write and vote on laws without having to solely depend on representatives to write the laws. This then brings into question what is the reason for a representative government if power naturally leads to corruption, but other than this change to our system of government, the people are going to need a new source of reliable knowledge from whence they gain their inspiration to stand and express the type of society they wish to live in.

Healthcare

In many first and third world countries, healthcare is a joke, but there are positive advancements that certainly deserve some reputation. But even in countries where healthcare is nationalized, there are very big discrepancies that are suppressed because of a certain narrative that science has been bent on in order to get back at religion. There have been often suppressed technologies that have healed many people from severe forms of cancer because it would hinder the profits certain companies can make from regular forms of medicine. There is said to be a text dating back thousands of years that revealed all the ways in which a human being could be healed from any type of disease and one of the attributed symbols of the author of said text is to this very day heralded as the insignia of all modern medicine as the caduceus.

Based on the materialistic approach, the diseases oftentimes as the case for a common medical issue are not properly understood despite the cure seeming to help the patient in the short term. But what is not recognized is the study of energy dynamics and in part string theory is on to something here, but the approach of considering how there is an immaterial cause for all material effects. This consideration is quite threatening to modern medicine because it would require a new foundation in which to base all diseases and then how to perhaps treat them if the cause isn't dealt with. The saying is that if the wound is not disinfected, applying the bandaid will only make the situation worse and applies for the consideration that materialized medicine has the system backwards.

There are many medical advancements that should still be used to treat diseases, but the way in which we fully undergo healing needs to be reconsidered if we are to increase trust in the medical industry. There are a couple different sides to view this next statement, but one of them is already circulating the world and it is the nationalization of healthcare, the declaration that healthcare is a right is a move in the positive direction because many people cannot afford to see a doctor or pay for a treatment even if they do have insurance. There doesn't need to be the privatized middle man of insurance companies making a huge profit in a world where there is enough wealth to give everyone the right to free healthcare.

Lastly, there are many pharmaceutical companies who fund various studies into whether certain drugs are beneficial to people when those same companies often have a top down model of profits gained to allocate on top. This is a controversial incentive that underwrites actual trust and value derived from the companies themselves and will further lead to social disparagement if outside sources aren't prioritized to evaluate the reliability of such drugs. The last concern with the use of drugs to treat psychological illness is quite faulty at the start given the nature of what the psyche actually is. The continued use of such treatment on a person's mental health as if the psyche is a purely biological component will only allude to repeat various disorders that are in line with the current increase in psychological disorders despite pharmaceutical treatment.

The fact that one can be born in a nice family and grow up in a nice community without much crime and still be prone to get depressed or resort to the use of drugs shows that there is more to the human life than a materially approved system that so far is only generating more degenerative conditions for those currently living through the world around them.

Infrastructure

One of the biggest concerns in this arena has often been related to the suburban sprawl that requires community members to commute long distances in order to go to work. Another concern is the price of housing increasing for the average residential home due to the increase in square feet. Cities have turned many districts into sectors of subsidized funding for special aesthetics to meet the fashion trend of modern luxury. Cities have been known to take taxes from suburban poor areas and designate the budget to those areas that have more wealth. The way many cities are built is quite inhumane considering the incentives of not just the types of businesses in place which are often bureaucratic and profit-focused but the arrangement and style of the buildings are often repetitive and ignorant of the necessity for ecological integration.

People may not see the need to have more biodiversity in cities or even suburban areas, but if you look at the physique of most modern communities, there is an exceptionally boring and ugly standard that doesn't presume higher diversification is important. Biodiversity is a huge pillar for ways to make everyday life look interesting because of the patterns and geometries that plants have being so unique and symmetrical at the same time. Creating buildings with all sorts of weird shapes isn' t necessarily going to guarantee a beautiful expression of diversity. When the average person walks through a city or even a suburb, there is often very little connection one has to the natural world because in these very urbanized areas there are often very little incentives for community connection and cooperation. In nature trees have a system where the roots communicate with each other known as a mycorrhizal network and I feel human beings long to have a similar way of understanding one another.

I know in nature there is infighting between animal and insect species but there is also a lot of order built in between various species that forms a congruent evolution whereas the trend in westernized societies but also anywhere else forms often a profit driven incentive versus a human base. This is one of the reasons why many people intuitively feel that many urbanized localities are not serving the needs of human welfare but I am not saying to get rid of these areas but rather consider reforming them. I do realize there is a certain level of expertise in planning and development, creating architecture blueprints and various things but these fields are quite materialized which is why sacred geometry, a bit of a superstitious phrase but when investigated will further designate what some european

communities are already doing in relation to
ecological and humanitarian integration.

It is my understanding that in the future new
industries and technologies will surface allowing a
completely new model of urban development to exist.
Ideas on how manipulating the atomic structure of
any material item when put through a 3D printer
could very well outpicture an exponential quantum
leap to where a whole house or building can be
created from just a small element. This suggests an
entirely new technology that science isn't so
interested in funding but this coincides with the new
technology that will uproot in the foreseeable future
that will no longer require fossil fuels.
Antigravitational technology is coming and this could
be one way on how modern day commutes don't
have to be a thing to stress about due to the pile of
traffic, accidents, and long travel times because
airways would exponentially knock off the limited
space required to get from one destination to
another.

Military

This institution is a complete farce given the nature of how free will works which is that whenever you do something unto another, you will receive back what you send even in the action of self-defense. The idea that one's life can be lost if the body is killed is created from a long timespan of narcissistic ideologies that has to this day developed a very material understanding of an immaterial universe. The nature of our current paradigm incites fear that one must epically do whatever is necessary unto another person in order to save their life is one of the pillars of the military. The other pillar results in the idea that we are separated from a universal source that created everything and everyone and so the idea of killing another person will not affect the source from which that person came because our modern belief is that there is no real intelligent source from which people are born.

Down through the millenniums and even suggested beyond recorded history, there has been a drive for power and control through militant dominance which has to this day created a fear-based society where huge industries have prospered to thus threaten others that death is real and must be considered real otherwise others will kill us. But this is a circular ideology that was created for only one thing and that is to create mass suffering so that certain individuals who created this premise could gain pleasure. The reason why these individuals gain pleasure from creating suffering upon both sides of any given conflict cannot be explained by any rational or logical means unless we were to consider an immaterial universe and the operations from which this universe may exist. Science has no interest in considering such a reality because then it would reverse its foundation of the random creation story to that of being non random but quite based on intelligence itself which would then cause many identifications with our current view of the world to change, most assuredly our view of killing.

Certainly the military has been known to be the proprietor of various human inventions and advancements of our time, but who is to say that these advancements would have already come about if huge timelines of humanities history hadn' t been dedicated to killing others? It is incredibly reasonable to say that the military may very well be the leading progenitor to delay and or destroy humanitarian advancements due to the foundational mission being 100% out of alignment with how reality actually works.

The military spending that goes on throughout nations coincided with a stock market casino allows wealthy individuals to further exploit and fracture the

essential rights everybody has to a decent standard
of living and a world where peace is the unilateral
reality. The focus or tactic on creating bigger armies
and stronger weapons is used in such a way to instill
greater fear in people that they will suffer more if
they do not comply with the demands of any given
nation using killing as a justification for peace, even
if it' s to kill another person who wants to lead a
nation's army to kill the entire world. This plan
would be exponentially thwarted non-violently if
there was a leading majority of people that stands
for non-violence and non-fear in the advent of death
being an illusion. But since the dawn of empires,
fear of death based on the idea of a universal
unintelligent source has been the means to get people
to react through the highly fluctuation of stimulated
pain on the physical body to manipulate the free will
decision and understanding of the intelligent soul
within the body.

Justice

Punishment does not in any way help a person feel connected to a higher form of identity or worldview but the reason our system is so bent on this form of adjudication is because our history again, has been carried out by tyrants who know how inflicting pain can not only control the everyday decisions on people but on how they can obtain pleasure. Criminals, thiefs, robbers, and serial killers, even terrorism, are all results of a historical chain reaction of dictatorships which is a form of narcissism. The institution to police, fine, arrest, and incarcerate individuals is built on the back of a social system that suggests there is a finite appropriation of resources and that we must use brute force to excavate these limited resources ensures a level of trust to the individual whereby they deserve more resources. But this system is unstable because whether from the beginning or the end, human disconnection ensues to shape the view of the world in such a way where competition versus cooperation is the model to place our trust.

The system of laws, lawyers, judges, and due process is incredibly incoherent given the understanding the collective masses have on what free will is or means. I know I cannot fully explain it here, but the idea that an individual could do something wrong when the very mechanics of that individual allows them to express their conscience as they see fit alludes to the idea of a faulty system of evolution or even creation. I realize just because I write this, the system of law and order is not going to go away, nor do I think it's healthy to just remove this system as a population that is vastly uneducated on the mechanics of free will will result in a type of anarchy which would then give credence to autocrats to use inhumane forces at their disposal.

For the time being, the incarceration system will not change but the way we give second chances can change, but this would require an evolution in the industry of mental health or psychology to consider immaterial and systemic factors for why people choose to break a law. It is very important that there are services for helping incarcerated people get a second chance, helping them to experience inspiration from the sense that they are worthy to have a decent standard of living and that there are plenty of resources in order to give them what they need to live without having to slave their life to some company that doesn't care about their spiritual and financial wellness.

Part of the reason crime exists is because psycho-spiritual classes are taught in school growing up, classes that give students tools for how they can resolve various difficult experiences that may happen

to them and this is another reason why people find it
so difficult to resolve matters in between themselves
without appealing to authority. The reasons why
courtrooms are so judgemental and hypocritical of
individuals whether they are innocent or guilty is
because there is a big gap in between people' s
ability to differentiate how their ego can manipulate
the opinion of others when the true goal is not to
convince anyone of anything but rather present
alternative ways in which both sides can meet an
agreement. So in the future it should be considered
that people will have a higher understanding on how
to resolve issues and how judges can be better
trained to understand how individual and systemic
ignorance can create further conflicts that are often
petty and inconsequential.

Technology

Technology is a byproduct of consciousness and the consciousness that goes into the technology will be reliable according to the principles in which that consciousness stands. In the world of technology, there are many intelligent people but there has been a deterrence from principles which is also affecting technology. Pretty simple to understand but the principles in which I speak give acknowledgement to the current state of affairs which are somewhat obvious and somewhat not obvious but many technology companies are currently disinterested in building technology away from exploitative data mining, decentralizing platforms, and making transparent company wealth and transactions.

It's pretty amazing what technology can do today given the level of awareness people had a century ago, but it still hasn't reached a level where it has really shaken the world into what is really going on. Certain whistleblowers have been able to make great use of technology in various ways, but for the average person it doesn't seem like it can really be a tool to support the livelihood of others because the average person doesn't feel equipped nor educated on what really they can talk about to bring awareness to how beliefs can exploit, harm, and cause violence. The majority of people understand how religious beliefs can harm people, but as religion fades a new industry of manipulation will begin to surface and we are only at the tip of the iceberg given what artificial intelligence can do.

Certainly there will be more to talk about as robots are normalized around daily life causing the interpersonal relationships that humans can have using A.I. but at the current moment general forms of addiction need to be addressed with more priority. Removing video games that involve killing, removing pornography, and removing any other forms of extreme content causing body euphoria or adrenaline rush will not eliminate the problem causing addiction. Certainly killing people for fun and body objectification are big issues but no issue will be resolved through erasing or blocking built-in human archetypes. So what needs to be done are conversations that technology encourages to be had where it isn' t just people talking about whatever they want all the time but there are existential incentives to remove worldwide human suffering from the basis of these platforms.

Technology will go through many challenges in the years to come when it comes to censorship and the solution will only get easier as platforms decentralize allowing less pressure to be so topheavy causing extreme pendulum swings that can form a risk to sensitive and immature individuals that would otherwise be able to see content that would also be extreme. Doom scrolling is a condition happening with short videos that many platforms have been quick to create so they can hyper-extract personal trends or data to further filter social demands to be profitable and attention grabbing. This issue will be important for tech companies as a means to opening deeper conversations on how we don't get caught in feeling the addiction to keep scrolling "forever".

Garden walling is not a concept I am good at memorizing but in simple, it's the condition where social media companies make it really difficult for infamous people to connect with each other which easily creates a parasocial simulator where participants come into the network bubble seeing trends and popular content versus content created with low attention or "social acceptance".

Parenting

Not everyone is fit to be a parent which is why many children are abused, neglected, and have no real sense of purpose in life, which is why a certain process should examine the psycho-spiritual background of a given individual or couple that want children. Right now there is too much pressure on parents to raise their children in a direction that gives them a higher form of purpose, which is why there is a saying that it takes a village to raise a child. With all the diverse conditions currently outplaying themselves on the planet, no two individuals can give a child a complete example on how to navigate life. Plus there is the added stress of maintaining a living that parents put up with that has heavy costs if it is an exploitative job because that means the child ends up receiving a certain end of the burden indirectly. Parents should not have to worry about finances in a world where the resources to go around are plentiful if society makes use of suppressed technologies by the elite class.

Never before has there been more divorces in westernized nations because of a historical tradition known as gender roles which is largely at fault but not completely for the fragmentation of families. The idea that the man has more authority than the woman is a lie that has long ties to narcissistic theocracies. This has created many archetypes whereby a man feels entitled to be sexual pleased or abusively forceful in order to maintain the belief system of a strong man is what leads the family household. There are many other ideas out there denoting the opposite effect on the side of women, but there is also the big one that it is up to the woman to take care of the house and children which is subsiding a bit today as both partners are often having to work to meet the demands of survival.

As children and teens are furthermore susceptible to the shortcomings of modern day technology and psycho-spiritual security, giving the youth a greater capture into the dark corners of the internet, blocking off websites and restrictive rules from being able to access the internet will not necessarily be the answer. It may help at certain intervals but what is really important is keeping the son or daughter in the know about the manipulative tactics happening in the world. The average citizen in the western world is not aware or educated on how there are many forces trying to steer the world away from a universal path of creative cooperation and optimistic encouragement. The rolling thunder in today' s world in the domain of manipulative tactics involves hypersexualization, indiscriminate violence, and extreme projections of dark humor that often catches the most vulnerable to find contention with.

So it can be said that it's never been harder
to raise a child in a world like this one, and there
very well may not be one type of school, program,
mentor, or parent that can adequately support the
needs of the collective unconscious that a child will
certainly take on. That is why communities, families,
neighborhoods, are going to start needing to work
together more to really support one another, and this
also goes for adults because we are all truly children
inside who have innocence that can be so easily
stripped and stomped on. So we can say that a
greater need for cooperation but also transparency
will be needed on what information is being
exchanged between the youth, information that will
be vital to help evolve conversations that bring
maturity versus division.

Abortion

So what is there to resist about giving birth to a baby, well in ethics there really isn't much because babies, despite the maintenance and cleanup, are incredibly wondrous or filled with wonder given their consciousness is in such a pure state, they are so easily prone to the world's greatest subtleties which can be the best or worst scenario. There is another side of ethics that takes into account the desire for independence and free time for self-exploration that can be incredibly difficult to attempt while having children. But sometimes one thing leads to another and ignorance takes its toll on a couple creating a situation where a baby can very well be a soon to be reality that wasn't something desired by the pair. This is where current technology comes in to be able to abort the baby which has caused a big uproar for traditionalists who have come to believe in a worldview very much dependent upon ancient times. There is nothing inherently wrong with this, but there are some definite side effects that causes further entropy within often conservative leaning pro-life groupings.

There may very well be an argument on where life starts and for people all over the world people to narrow in on where it might be but surprising enough this is often a scapegoat conversation for the issue that comes with having a child in a capitalist dictatorship whereby parents have very little recourse to sustain themselves which includes their wellness in a marketplace dominated by greed, corruption, and aggressive exploitation. Adding to this fact, government assistance is little to be found through the advent of needing financial assistance to take care of the basic needs of the child(s). This is a major problem especially if there is a breakup in the parents which could very well jeopardize the standard of living for the parents involved which can mean various things that are never really taken into consideration by traditionalists.

So despite nations especially in america that are on the verge to try to put an end to various forms of abortion, it can mean that certain economic sectors can start to wobble and fracture other compartments of society, especially if the parents involve really begin to lose their sense of self or mental health. But if we look deeper into the abortion issue, what we really find behind the traditionalist view is trend of an ethnically white and often male appropriated constituent of power. The decisions by these white men often have no clue what women have to go through to raise a child especially if we are going to consider traditionalist trends to normalize gender roles that give superiority to the father figure. The other factor here is that most of these men in powerful positions that argue against abortion have lots of wealth, and this wealth throughout time has served as a highwall to prevent empathetic feelings of what suffering parents or single parents that are often women have to go through.

It is a given knowledge that children and teens should be properly prepared to know what they are dealing with whenever the have sexual relations but at the same time certain over the counter medication is available to prevent an abortion from happening. Sometimes this doesn' t work in time and that is why the couple should be as informed as possible before they probably become a couple but another factor in all of this is that treatment should be free. Abortions can be quite costly and significantly render a couple in an impoverished place if the government isn' t willing to consider their power and distribute free support.

Firearms

Right now it's very understandable given our history that the worldview most people have still has a disconnect between the justification to kill and how that perpetuates a force to kill us. Even in self-defense people are sending or standing on an idea that suggests the results of what happens to others does not in turn happen to them. This idea is very old and continues to propagate various types of fuel to various types of conflict, be it nations or individuals. As nations continue to raise their general awareness, it will become harder and harder to justify why we need weapons given how the worldview begins to change based on longer periods of peace. The funny thing about creating a law to remove the right to bear arms is difficult to absolve with the current mindset that sees that only through the use of force or punishment can we reprimand citizens.

It's quite obvious that people are not ready to give up their justifications for killing others, especially in the united states given that so many do not believe they would be harming themself if they are taking the life of another away. People justify often in fear that a criminal or government might try to take away their life that they then can use the same tactics back upon another although it has been

said that an eye for an eye makes the whole world
blind. The fear people have of losing their life goes
way way back in time, a point in time where critics
would try to devour me for stating but nevertheless
originates to a time when in fact there was no death.
Since this time long ago, there has been a collective
identity to suggest that people should identify with
their body for who they are.

This worldview was reinforced many times
over through people in positions of power trying to
use the physical body as a scare tactic to get people
to do what they want. I know this goes against
modern epistemology or science as some might say,
but in many cases modern skeptics cannot fathom
another worldview because many of their built-in
ideas are rooted in the same divisive construct that
religion was built around with a much upgraded
software. This software again suggests we don't
have a soul and that the actions taken upon others
won't come back to that person. This is simple
energy dynamics and people will continue to receive
instances where a criminal, enemy, or nation might
threaten them as long as they continue to believe
their life solely depends on the outcome of their
body. This fear that there can't be another reality
blocks a non-violent reality from manifesting itself in
the world.

A very similar topic to the military and is a
topic that may be around for a little while longer

until people have had enough of their current sense of identity being limited versus unlimited. Whether through conflict or peace, there will be a much more progressive understanding in the coming years that sees other people as a part of themself. In the meantime of extreme events suggesting that a person might die from the use of a gun, any fear that people use in response will only delay this understanding of how connected we are already, and that there is no real reason to want to destroy the body of another person unless we want ours destroyed. Any reason for doing this you might say most probably won' t be able to be found because it' s entirely illogical to believe in this. So if guns are to be outlawed as a law it should outlaw all guns of any such government or nation and any infracture of this should be met with psycho-spiritual help or incarceration for criminal activity.

Narcissism

It will be some time before humanity understands how narcissism is created or at least how we understand that this is not a biological or genetic effect. Right now all we know is that they exist and have certain strategies oftentimes to seek out greater ways to enrich themselves or hurt others. Certain serial killers or psychopaths have been known to do what they do without any logical reason with our current understanding of how individuals are created, not necessarily through birth. As awareness continues to increase about narcissism, new protocols and documents will need to be created and or updated in order for certain outcomes in government but in all other areas of society cannot be compromised like it is right now.

It is possible to create certain types of psycho-spiritual tests to determine whether an individual is fit for a position of power using various technologies to monitor biological reactions to real world simulations. Certain questions may be easier for some narcissists to handle which is why the test facilitator should also have impromptu structures built into the test whereby the critical thinking skills of the tester becomes more transparent. At this current time the public majority is not educated enough on how the narcissistic psyche actually works so there is no way for something like this to work right now.

Narcissism is a subject that should be built somewhat into psycho-spiritual studies in school giving students a general awareness of how society has been built and how there may very well be narcissists inside positions of power in various parts of the world. Narcissism will be something that eventually goes away for various reasons but some of which is because the public majority has demanded essential rights from their government which won't allow certain leaders to exploit the population for self-centered interests.

One of the last blockades narcissists face especially in leadership positions is a more direct form of democracy which will help usher in a more transparent economic state allowing people to see various transactions and bank statements from those who are facilitating positions of power. People will find it easier to vote on specific leaders when monetary operations are made transparent but this will undergo major resistance in many forms that will try to polarize public opinion causing friction amongst citizen communication.

In the meantime, it is important for people to go out of their way to research narcissisology or elitism and how repetitive social ideologies have been reinforced to this day justifying why there isn't a sufficient number of resources on this planet to sustain 10 billion people with a decent standard of living. Also the idea that the average person isn't fit for leadership positions because they lack intellectual sophistication is another one. There are many ideas out there built into every area of society but the area people find most troubling lies between bureaucratic and academic criticism. This is because narcissists know it's easier to hide in darkness and most of the correspondence between these institutions are completely mental, lacking major interest to get to the heart, to get to the center of human suffering with a knowledge of how historical narcissism works.

No better way to avoid self-criticism than to justify the grounds of scientific materialism as the ultimate authority just like how the roman catholic church justified its grounds that reinforces a social class divide, a divide that naturally creates a sense that one person is more valuable than another person because they agreed to the current ideology at the time.

Transparency

Right now many big platforms get us to sign or agree to a contract of terms and conditions that give them a right to own and sell our data for profit. Many people understand what they are doing when they agree to a contract but people don't understand is their power to boycott, organize, and demonstrate essential rights to have a market free of cyber monopolies that hide their actual actions underneath the surface of sophisticated communication technology. While all this is going on, another domino is being struck without public awareness and that is the income inequality that is processed to those in the higher ups and the shareholders. Aside from tax evasion that many wealthy people do, there is a very limited area of access to important information about where large sums of money go and how it's used. If employees and customers really knew how more and more money is being funneled in the hands of fewer and fewer individuals, there would be more motivation to stand up in resistance.

The problem here is not just which social media giants but it goes into every sector of society where people at the top are making the rules where it should be unilateral. Because of the lack of democratic engagement, we have enabled a ruling class of so-called leaders to enact justice and reform

when in fact they are only wanting to increase their
self-interest. But as I stated before, the lack of
democratic engagement has many branches to how
this situation came about and it has been going on
for a long time. Tables have turned with the advent
of the internet and people being able to access
progressive ideas and sources of knowledge but this
has also in many ways fired back because of the
overwhelming sources of false information and or
sources of plain old distraction entertainment that has
leveraged our historical inferiority to cope.

The right to privacy that the wealthy use is
often justified by the right to privacy that the
average person is given for "cooperating" with the
contract. What people don't realize is that the
people at the top holding down inconceivable amounts
of wealth and power are projecting the existential
need for people to want their own privacy because
their information can be used to harass and violate
their life. Most people really don't care if their
private life was revealed on the internet with the
exception of sex activity and bathroom utilities but
because people have bought into the lie that we need
full and complete privacy, the echelons have justified
their trench they have dug in saying they don't
need to reveal anything about their life, their bank
accounts, transactions, and company strategies.

Social media giants outpicture the face of an
economy rampant with this privacy charade to hide

the power and privileges of the elite. In the
foreseeable future, especially over this next decade,
more demands for whistleblowers will arise causing
more public disagreement over their use of social
media that will lead for more organizations to
demand not just new decentralized companies but also
a decentralized government in the coming decades.
Right now there are big legal hurdles to jump
through but as time and social distrust increase, the
power these hurdles have to stop people from
demanding essential rights for ubiquitous
transparency to be legislated. This move will be
colossal for the reformation of a more direct form of
democracy but cannot be achieved without this public
outcry for complete transparency over how big
companies are using people for their own paradise.

Housing

There is enough resources and energy to give
everyone proper housing but this statement is
rebutted very quickly through mainstream economic
analyses and resource industries because the claim is
there is a only a finite amount of resources and
certain national players would be selfish to think they
can receive more than what they can afford to pay
for. Right now in the modern democracies the
average median home is built at 4000 sq feet which
is unnecessary for decent living conditions as people
can live well off in a 1000 square foot home. If
someone wants to have more kids and wants a bigger
home they should have to pay for the extra privileges
whereas the essential rights for everybody should be
paid for because there is enough wealth and
resources.

The idea that those who have billions have a
right to not distribute their wealth is criminally
incompetent to the paradigm of that everyone
deserves a decent standard of living for the harm
that comes with not having adequate securities is
devastating. The idea that certain enriched
individuals can have more assets and wealth than
they would ever need in their entire life is criminal
and will be reproached in the upcoming years.
Universal basic housing will be criticized for making

people lazy and resort to a life of someone who does nothing and resorts to behavior that costs communities more to upkeep is a lie. As more people are given basic securities that suggest someone is valued in this world, the more people are willing to find value in themselves and share that with the world. But right now the majority of people need various types of rehabilitation due to the extreme divide they have with knowing themselves.

The foreseeable future is not going to have a point where everybody stops working in order to share their gift they are here to bring to the world, but everybody will be offered various programs to help them reintegrate with the principles of nature, the universe, and especially their conscience that all requires no competition in order to expand intelligence let alone civilization. As robotics and artificial intelligence expand into industries, more free time will be available to the average person to live as they please with their home completely available without fear or threat that they could be homeless due to loss of payment.

Alongside with new types of infrastructure that will enable people to live a much more creative life in their neighborhood, housing infrastructure or neighborhoods should include community recreational activities and gardens. At the current time it is much more reliable to build housing near areas of business but with westernized development and planning, a steep degradation of social values has mirrored the inefficiency of current creations. As new sources of energy and technology allow for easier commute times with little cost, suggesting flying cars is coming to reality, people find more appreciation in developing a community spirit of cooperation, allowing for the whole paradigm of housing and neighborhoods to be reimagined in a much more positive light.

When people are given basic housing which is not threatened by a competitive capitalist market based on materialism, they have much more self-esteem and value to engage with others around them. With basic housing everyone should be able to receive basic furnishings without added necessities for free leaving people to spend their own money on things that are unnecessary. Who decides what is necessary versus unnecessary will come through a more direct form of democracy, but essential shelter is a reality absolutely coming.

Employment

There is never a limited or lack of job opportunities but with the current worldview there is a very limited understanding of how energy works or how energy is produced. For a long time, people have grown up with the idea that you must force nature to give you what you want by cutting a tree, mining ore, sowing seeds and various other means to produce material that is deemed valuable, but at the same time another type of technology has always existed that allows for people to mold the world around them according to the conscience versus trying to force materials together through hard labor. It's even a bit rude to call this a technology because it's actually a built in code or law through which one has the ability to imagine or use imagination. Right now the only purpose of materialism is to show people that there is definitely a tough way to live life, but that is only because we have accepted a certain narrative or story about who we really are which is often distorted through various means, one being through historical narcissism.

The entire world economy is about to boil over and burst the floodgates due to the long trend of ignoring basic realities to how human beings can live without much of the current systems currently in place. The stress and anxiety levels of each person is

shooting through the roof due to a lack of questioning
how our current paradigm operates under a force
based dynamic that produces our material conditions.
New industries are more ready now than ever for
how we can process a new worldview into conditions
that give everyone a decent standard of living. The
current establishment is unwilling to consider this
worldview because they want to see this new world
before the enactment of different ideas put forth
through experimentation.

As money is consolidated further and further
to fewer and fewer individuals, people will naturally
want to organize a democratic model within their job
so their stress and anxiety can cease to exist on
large levels. There is so much tension at work due to
the inclination one might have to do something
healthy for their body while withstanding conditions
that have little to no empathy for the health of
one's body. How long a person can stand for, when
a person needs to eat, when someone just needs to
take a break, when someone can go to the bathroom
are often built on industries that rely upon
force-based mechanics to produce the desired
product. Many scientists and experts will criticize me
because I'm not showing proof of a non-force based
model to create products but proof can't be shown in
a fraction of time considering the engineering our
minds have gone through to believe that our
imagination can't give us what we need. Yet there

have been people separated from charlatans throughout the world who have demonstrated that our mind has the capacity to defy the laws of physics.

Furthermore the job market will take on a huge new wave of creativity and play in the coming decades and the timespan will only shorten so long as capitalist views of market maneuverability grow in distrust which will certainly happen as market crashes are inevitable. New freedoms from the employees will drastically change allowing them to have a much wider connection with customers whereby they are no longer seen as consumers but as human beings. The level of communication will drastically surge between people because there is no longer the hustle to squeeze out profits to fill the whims of someone who takes no care for those who are barely making it mentally, emotionally, and physically. This will help fuel untapped potentials for a market without force-based technology to generate a supply for all to have.

Basic Payment

Along with basic housing, this is another thing that will meet heavy opposition due to the level of distrust of the individual currently in the collective worldview. This distrust has been built over a long time of believing in the force-based model for how the world works, giving in to the archetypes of the narcissists that have worked quite successfully but don't realize they have been losing their basic humanity of general care for another. Either way basic trust will be reignited into humanity whether through peace or chaos, but it can be accelerated as more awareness is brought to the table on how we as individuals are inherently good and don't wish harm upon others. Certainly with the knowledge of narcissists we realize that they think very differently and don't wish good upon others so much but as time goes on we will see how they were not always like this and how there is a slight chance they can change their heavily cemented worldview.

As stated in basic housing, people will think that their taxes, which is another arguable subject about trust being given to the individual, will be a waste or rather go towards some result that will fuel further degradation of society. The part many of these people fail to realize is that these people who might spend their basic payment on drugs or entertainment that has very little creative output are often already psycho-spiritually ill. I'm refraining from saying psychologically ill because this term has turned into a purely mental construct when in fact it mostly relates to one's soul. People who have no trust in who they are or their creative capacities to enrich people's lives that help bring in diverse experiences that further the sense of an interconnected humanity have often been historically engineered to believe in the matrix. Yes, very much like the movie where this is this simulated "well organized" world between the average person and the elite.

In order for people to become well in heart, mind, and soul, various new shifts will have to take place that not only put a stop to the extreme wealth gap but also to implement rehabilitation facilities especially in nature to help people decompress from the day in an day out hustle of survival or competition based realities. Over time nature will eventually reintegrate into modern populations but in the meantime there will be an ecological divide for most urban and suburban areas strickening the sense of a higher and symmetrical pattern in life is absent. Certainly the rollout of this world I'm painting sounds like a much better world or some might call it a utopia but I still see challenges and conflicts but just with much less extremism and frequency.

The basic payment will allow people to travel more and meet people who they wouldn't normally meet through their everyday routine. Certainly not everyone is going to abandon their job in order to travel because most people realize things would fall apart if we just all of a sudden switched everything overnight, it would be chaos and people need time to consider and collaborate based on these ideas to come to their own conclusions and perhaps bring in ideas to help fill in the gaps of our modern divided state. Plus it will be apparent that there are people who deeply need more free time to find themselves before applying for any serious position in life because if they are to go about their life with a fractured sense of self they will only be hurting others in the process and many of these people are impoverished or homeless today.

Banking

I think many people feel the unnecessary reliability we have for banks not just as individual companies but as an institution. Many people realize that most transactions that go on in daily life are through an online network that credit and debit cards offer but yet the necessity for physical banks to provide physical security in that people might steal your physical money is obsolete with current technology. It is very much possible for the government, private companies, or non-profit organizations to build online spaces whereby people can access their account and participate in transactions without having the fundamental mechanism of the entity make money off of money. The only argument banks have in the creation of interest fees, mortgage contracts, and loans is that people are not inherently moral or creative aspiring to generate positive effects in the world.

The banking institution is based on fear in itself, that we live in a world where we should fear others because they might take value that is not otherwise recognizable from the accepted legal tender. I can talk at length about why there is even a need for currency all because human beings have lived through countless ages whereby the worldview is based on a disconnected universe which begets a disconnected race. But given the currencies we have today, it is well recognized that a digital form of currency is on the horizon and certainly bitcoin and the other cryptocurrencies are valid forms of currency given the whole process of mining is asymmetrical with how true value is assigned to any given product or service.

The banking intuition is actually an industry that pumps and validates large sums of economic value to those who have no real intention of providing value into the economy other than their pseudo-intellectual sophisticated worldview that will always support the capital materialist model of the world that allows them to legalize criminality. There is a lot to be done within this industry and a lot can happen quick as many people realize the absolute incompetence it has with any universal principles that deal with supporting humanity from the bottom up, not the top down.

So whatever is to happen to this industry, it should be made known that people who are wanting to create businesses that have a positive creative impact should be supported without strings after a certain vetting process has made clear that the person(s) actually have positive interests even if the business doesn' t work out. So many businesses are created for the wrong reasons today because of this model of for profit success and all this does is circlejerk the industry to justify what they are doing because capitalism in its core is all about beating, winning, and plain old exploiting.

The one thing that should be made clear is that there will always be an option for somebody to start a business if they have an idea and that there will always be available funding for a business idea with a positive incentive. The idea that you can only give funding to those who are adequate to semi-moderately surviving capitalism because they are either finding ways to exploit others in masked ways or that their "ingenuitive" strategy is to luxuriously falsify trends that have little value to real world novelty or humanity is criminal and headed to the dustbin. Philanthropy has often served as a mask for those who wish to exponentially exploit people and is something already being critically exposed. Removing world poverty will not come through donating money but through funding models without prioritizing profit over people.

Government

Governments are never the issue when it comes to societal breakdowns because the main issue is always the ideas upheld by certain leaders. It can definitely seem like governments are big issues and it is indeed true that various governments around the world operate from a system that is extremely hierarchical which is not not in keeping with the democratic trends of today. Certainly it should be known that all forms of government are temporary models only existing to organize and demonstrate worldviews no matter how brutal or humanitarian. The reason why so many governments today are lacking the efficiency to provide safety and security of their people is because it has been a constant trend throughout history that the narcissistic elite have engaged with the public more than the love based leaders have.

So today we have most if not all governments that contain a majority base that has very little consideration for the wellness of the weakest members of society and so if we are wanting to see change in our government we must seek to understand why so many true leaders have abstained from involving themselves. One of the biggest reasons is based on a historical fear of being beaten and put down and then believing their self worth equates to whatever physical and public humiliations are taken from an attempt to show there is another way to bring the light. This memory lingers with many mature and humanitarian leaders but yet times have moved on in most nations whereby physical punishment cannot be the result of one speaking out. Unless you have insider information that heavily magnifies deep infractions within the government.

The government of the future will go through various hurdles that will be hard to predict, but some of the biggest ones deal with potential civil wars and or artificial intelligence as nation conflicts are going to be subsiding given that more awareness of how energy works and is obtained will deflate the scarcity for resources and individual survival. As greater social movements demand more transparency amongst the political divide, bigger systems will need to be erected to include larger groups of trustworthy representatives. As the population continues to increase to 10 billion, more leadership representatives will be necessary to fully communicate the diverse array of challenges humanity will face whereby maintaining a very small elect group to be the mouthpieces of humanity will grow incompetent. But the stress factor on representatives will lessen as the democratic system changes to allow people to write and pass laws without consent of the representative body.

The reason to have representatives in government is not only to be a space of inspiration for the people but also to help organize and strengthen government compartments that deal with the public, helping to officiate the citizen members or employees of the state to best carry out their job. As violent conflict or threats of war begin to subside, new industries within the government will be augmented to allow the people to finally have a fear free decent standard of living that fulfills the declaration that life, liberty, and the pursuit of happiness is completely enacted. Right now there is so much hypertension and inertia built around surveillance, drugs, terrorism, and any form of criminal activity that it literally removes space from governments being able to successfully help the majority have a decent standard of living. The premise that we can prevent or punish others for crimes with violent measures is not actually solving the problem but cleverly reinforcing it.

Immigration

Immigration is generally a good thing because it shows there is value in the cultures of other people. Obviously with our current state of affairs, people would not be able to adapt to immigration easily if large numbers of people from a certain country with a different culture and language were to integrate into society. In our current state, it is somewhat reasonable to provide security clearance at borders and airports to see if someone is smuggling drugs or weapons but what has often fueled the international war on drugs is the making of a substance illegal. Immigration does not have to be a big deal if there is a willingness of immigrants to learn the language of the country and try to understand how the country works. Right now though, it is difficult for people to understand how a country works and be productive because there is so much corruption and negligence going on from the top down, so this is one reason why immigration can be a very difficult thing.

One red flag that countries should be aware of is that immigrants often immigrate not because they are curious about how life works in another country but to escape conditions that do not favor essential rights of the individual. There is often a

reluctance of wealthy countries to ignore the
assistance that impoverished countries need and we
aren' t talking about philanthropy but we are talking
about trained leaders going into a country and
actually engaging in the public discourse.
Philanthropy can be tough to implement because
governments of third world countries are often
disinterested in the evolution of the people, this can
also go for organizations and charities as there are
many false representatives of supporting the public.

Immigration will begin to become more of an
international issue if third world countries are
unwilling to consider reforming themselves to better
the people front and center. So along with leaders
going in to help resolve the issues, there can be
leadership teams or committees who go into a country
not just with knowledge on how to move past the
issues but with funding to provide specific oversight
on where and how certain programs and sectors can
be boosted. Sending a bunch of money to a country is
not the answer if there are strong ties of that
government to corruption and divisiveness.

As the incoming future impedes, immigration
may get a bit flustered due to the rising social chaos
involving propaganda and identity politics causing
more security and fear towards immigration although
it will differ according to different parts of the
world. But the world will eventually see the
similarities we all hold that stretch beyond borders

which will allow much more tolerance of immigration from many parts of the world. With big countries like Russia, China, and India, it is possible there can be events where large amounts of people want to immigrate due to a clamping down of power and control. In the case of these events, nations will generally be more open to letting people in as long as religious terrorism remains miniscule to absent. These powers are unlikely to meet heavy resistance to other countries accepting them unlike countries in the middle east.

In regards to the middle east, it seems like they may require a little more time to reconcile their religious differences internally and internationally but with rising movements of progressive religious practices, there will be more openness to allow people from the middle east to immigrate to different countries.

Economics

From research, not necessarily economically based research, it seems as if the world of markets and currencies is a byproduct of a planetary experiment that took off at a certain period of time going way back beyond recorded history. During this time that I'm going to refrain from specifying even though there is evidence, it suggests that that humanity was at a level of intelligence that decided to mentally compartmentalize interactive behavior to such a degree that the decided way of learning was to judge people by their ability to analyze narratives for how to interpret the world as it is. As complex as this sounds, it has a specific connection to the complexity of our current economic system whereby the goods and services are all compartmentalized through the context of profit, pleasure, and competitive superiority.

Since the dawn of recorded history, civilization has gone through three different stages of economics all serving a purpose to help the people recognize what it is they really want but through a complicated lens of judging the production quality to determine the person's quality. This is a very rough way to build a civilization but this is one of the big lessons humanity is choosing to learn as it continues to compete against one another rather than see that

there are enough resources for everybody to live a
good life.

The first stages of economic development
amongst recorded history were bargain based whereby
everybody sort of determined the value for
themselves after the rulers got what they needed
because currency was more based on practical
necessities. The second stages were based on
command through the rulers themselves deciding
oftentimes which compartments of society should
receive special interest even though there was still
bargaining power, the currency shifted to precious
metals in the form of coin oftentimes manufactured
by the ruler. The third type of economy we have is a
mixed one whereby the supply of practical necessities
has outnumbered the demand for what people need
creating an imbalance between the corporate
government alliance and the common people even
though in reality there is no imbalance, just that
which we create with our minds.

So the next stage for the world economy will
take some time to complete but there will be a
necessity for people to understand why we are not
protesting the crimes the government is giving not
just to itself but to corporations allowing huge sums
of money to consolidate into the hands of fewer and
fewer people. Some people will need to understand
this history of how this kind of started from the
original bankers of medieval europe, some will simply

need to understand that what is happening today
isn't right and we have the right to demand a debt
free system that doesn't infatuate the pockets of
those who created the system. As a side note, the
people did allow this to happen but rather from an
unsuspicious level of conscience, so it's not entirely
the fault of the elite.

In the meantime, the necessity for people to
shift their attitude towards money will get harder as
the system pressures more people to believe in the
illusion of lack, poverty, and creative instability. But
as entrepreneurs venture away from profit driven
motives and as activists organize movements in
decent, the foreseeable future will create a much
more unified labor force that has rights, benefits,
and securities that have never before been seen in
history. The common term is that the democratization
of the business world will allow people to finally feel
free from the contracts of exploitation that have thus
far seemed insurmountable.

Bullying

A more obvious form of human expression that takes place at a young age even pre-teens that has a critical impact on the individual but yet still takes place often throughout one's adult life in a more indirect and dressed up way. With the internet, countless new ways of communicating harassment or judgment have surfaced to thereby expose the collective unconscious, the world mind that contains all identifications humans have with themselves. Growing up as a child into the teen years is the most severe experience or effect of bullying because the individual often has no conscious understanding of how people are unequal. Especially in western culture, it happens quite quickly with the types of games, toys, and relationships the parents give but also with how the parents treat themselves.

So it is often right away that the child is grown up with a certain standard for what beauty looks like, what strength or courage looks like, and so the end result is often contradictory with the basic worldview that we have more similarities than differences. Because children have different souls which have yet to be acknowledged by academia, the authority for what is deemed true or rather teachable, children have different drives for how they wish to express themselves within the standard of

cultural norms which are often toxic. The most
consequential bullying dynamic is related to gender
roles whereby males should express physical and
intellectual superiority and outcompete others around
them, especially those who are labeled as inferior or
weak. Females have a dynamic where they are
judged more heavily on their appearance than males
but they also have a pressured standard to be
superior intellectually just not as much as males. But
gender is another illusion which will be talked about
in the gender section.

The other aspect of bullying takes into
account the personalities which has overlays from
previously described characteristics but adds into the
mix humor, sex, and a little bit of passion or
creative ability. Everything that I'm writing is
obvious, I'm just making it more clear in words how
it can be described or expressed. Bullying is
leveraging the internet within these cultural
archetypes to an exponential degree to judge or
discriminate against others severely. This is causing
unprecedented levels of self-harm and trauma that
most definitely affects society as a whole and vastly
affects the morale and spirit of teams working in the
field but it will be the lower paid industries that
break down faster than those dressed up with nice
incomes.

There are many progressive trends that have
been inspired by LGTBQ, mental health, and spread

the love movements that have given more awareness
and support for people dealing with social conflict.
Mental health and suicide hotlines are an absolute
mess that many people have spoken anger about their
incompetence to be human but this government allied
healthcare system is steeped in centralized power
which disables intersectional holistic expressions to be
mentioned. Our healthcare system and the treatment
of those psychologically hurt does not meet the
standards for what human beings are going through
and so bullying is a multifaceted dynamic that
requires upgrades of awareness in many modern
fields of education but also production. So the trends
for youth instability that may be labeled as a type of
delusion from the older generation will increase but
in the long run will greatly transform some of the
massive blockades currently in place to suspend a
creative and supportive humanity.

LGTBQ+

    Humanities resistance to gender roles is finally coming to the surface and it is about time because that it happen because the countless tragedies and suffering this ideology of confining a person to a particular style of expression is not just inhumane but illogical given the nature of consciousness having so many interests to express diversity. The point of this movement to break away from historical identifications is not to build a new foundation in which people can be confined to another restrictive label but rather to show that we don' t inherently need worded identifications to merely express our conscience. The reason there has been great resistance to this movement is because there is great resistance to upgrade every part of society to a functioning humanity that empowers people versus exploits.

    The reason why we see an international power apparatus that is mostly governed by men is because of this very ideology of gender roles whereby men should be dominant and women submissive. People of the newer generations feel the vast disillusionment of this worldview and are beginning to comply less to the demands or ideas that do not give support or security or creative encouragement to express yourself in such a way that helps lower the division or violence that is now more aggressive than ever to take away the humanity in people. The people being born right now naturally want life on earth to be better and have strong instincts that life could be better, which is why the young generation are expressing themselves more and more diversely. This isn't to say that diversity is the answer to our problems but it is one facet that has been heavily repressed internationally because of this rather conservative but now unilateral professional filter that confines higher ranking positions to a very ancient tradition.

There has never been such a divide between worldviews that parents have in comparison to their children and it will continue to cause more friction amongst households as some already have gone so far to humiliate, punish, and abandon certain children disidentifying with normative traditions. Along these lines people of the resistance movement have attracted many forms of social disparity for their cause which has certainly take a toll in their lives as many of them are more prone to self-harm and attempting suicide. These social examples of cultural malfunction should be red flags to anyone in leadership positions with a sane mind to speak out about the harm of gender roles and how it can lead to the further breakdown of social sectors whereby the future will largely be operated by a young generation that has significantly higher numbers of identity diversification.

So what is to come from all this will vastly enhance ways people can express themselves without putting others down. This will trickle into industries currently unseen whereby economic value will surge extraordinarily in supply as the demand is only increasing. These new industries will not only attempt to use the metaverse or virtual realities as a means to radicalize mainstream narratives towards a non-violent spectrum of empathetic creativity but to incentivize autonomous reformations to democratize production and manufacturing facilities to absolve any punitive contracts on basic human health, wellness, and respect. The current system that is epitomized through corporate shoots and ladders has many hooks to threaten people who agree to work by suggesting oftentimes they are the selfish incompetent ones who may wish to go against various terms meant to squeeze out as much energy to satisfy the whimsy bank accounts of the few.

Voting

One of the most absolutely boring subjects because voting is so centralized, bureaucratic, and plain old too serious. We can all agree that voting is an important issue and should be taken with some seriousness as it does influence local, national, and world stage, but the level of importance it has on specific candidates as the representatives for how the world changes removes some of the empirical rights and principles that individuals need to see themselves already as leaders or examples. The quote out there is to be the change you wish to see in the world but when we put such pretension on that change coming from a few, then we begin to significantly erode the self-confidence of any given people. I am not saying that we need to do away with voting but the type of infrastructure in which voting is used and I'm not talking specifically about voting machines.

I might retract and say it's a bit more than infrastructure but I have mentioned about direct democracy in the politics section whereby people can make and vote on laws themselves without a representative crafting a law to institute. The idea that chaos would ensue because people don't have the knowledge to communicate vital social systems and degrees of expertise is laid on a very aristocratic tradition to always suggest the people don't know

best. Certainly the average person doesn't know
most of what there is to know in all specific fields
but the technology is here to help each other out on
how we can coordinate the building of our societies.
It is my understanding that the system of checks and
balances needs big upgrades and many of these
include many different committees of representation
amongst the public with user friendly technology that
allows easily accessible perhaps almost self-taught
systems much like certain website builders today that
allow very minimal learning curves.

I don't necessarily believe in term limits
because I believe the public knows best on when and
when not people should continue to hold office. But
surely mistakes will be made where the public knows
best but over the course of a long-term I trust the
public will know best by their quality of humanity
they have generally for one another. This is why a
new industry of trust and purpose (leadership) is
needed more than ever through the proliferation of
community organization and development, expanded
systems allowing more accessibility for one's voice
or ideas to be shared and discussed. The development
of prototypes and micro hubs for community and even
national coordination can scale without limit to allow
many more conversations and leaders to be born than
what most parliaments and governments institute.

Right now there is a massive hold on
government trust within communities to facilitate

programs of community leadership but also general education on how technology simulators can facilitate new ways of interacting governance through decentralized communities that could very well have cycles of centralization. Right now the pendulum swing is towards a type of anarchy or decentralization of everything when in fact it's still important to recognize leaders with ingenuitive or progressive ideas which is why trust recycling systems can allow micro hubs to turn into macro hubs but then restart over a period decided by the majority as a healthy process to examine unexplored spaces and leaders that would have never been given a chance for the spotlight. Through these new spaces and systems new relationships will be born within the individual to see more value in themselves and will in turn want to value others more, to simply trust more.

Media

As everyone knows, the media has never been more polarized despite there still being some rather progressive journalism out there. Even the progressives don't often have a bigger picture for what is going on as this would very much violate the current respected models of education that endorses the false narrative for who are we really and what is going on. But as the media in tandem with how identity politics works, will only be able to go so far in addressing material issues due to the cause of these issues coming from an immaterial source. Where is my evidence experts say, but the one who usually asks the question is often unwilling to search for serious answers that have been brought to the table most extraordinarily over the last 150 years. It is true once again that there have been many false examples or results that have given distrust to the knowledge of parallel universes and how the mind can tap into them to influence matter, but there still remains today a significant amount of proof that can be repeated over time.

The media as well all know is so focused on political matters because the echelons of science will not budge its stance on what subjects are worthy of investigation and what isn't. People might say if there were proven advancements the media would most certainly cover them but unfortunately slander and denial has poisoned the well of studying consciousness from being able to access funding and bipartisan critique. But as time goes on weird contractions will take place within the media including the alternative media which is still a relatively new phenomenon, contractions due to financial instability will pressure outlets to latch on to independent individuals covering the news as they see it. New approaches will be attempted to keep long standing popular media outlets alive but people will be less interested due to the increase in psycho-spiritual pseudoscience ignorance. This is the subject that conveys how there are more variables controlling the conditions that express themselves in what we call physical life.

The movement of spirituality sometimes combined with the term new age has made some progress as with some decline in terms of accuracy of knowledge being conveyed. It is true that the new age, psychedelic, and holistic movement that is somewhat combined with spirituality as a phrase is dominated by cognitive dissonance, a type of worldview that denies in large part evidence of individual responsibilities to engage in society in order for society to change. Many of these people think they don't need to learn about how society works and all they need to do is follow some coach, teacher, or psychic and apply their practices without communicating with people that have different beliefs in order to fulfill their calling. But as time goes on, more pressure will be applied with the cooperation of serious scientific investigation that will break through to aid in the social debate from being polarized between religion and science, democrat and republican, good and evil, light and darkness, the people and the government or corporations.

There is with all other industries, a large demand for a new type of media without ravening wolves syndrome, looking to use any material condition as a way to get back at the other socially established polarity that often forms its own ideology. In the coming times, new forms of media will arise seeking to express and expose how suffering, entropy, and collapse of the system is inherently tied into the collective worldview, the collective way at how we look at all life as interconnected whole versus a random mechanistic compilation of disconnected parts.

Environment

The topic where I'm going to get the most criticism is this one because greenhouse gas emissions don't lead to climatic weather problems, consciousness does. Now where is my evidence? The evidence would have already surfaced if there would have been funding to explore how consciousness works. Quantum mechanics has made progress but we are only at the tip of the iceberg. There is some information about the magnetic poles of the earth and how these poles are in constant communication with the magnetic poles of human beings. These poles can be related to the spinal column constituting sources of energy that the chinese and hindu peoples have known about for a long time. Westernized science has refrained from investigating seriously the behavior of energy sources undetectable to the human eye because it conflicts with the random-material origination for the universe.

There is no doubt that climate change is happening and that deniers of this are on a train to a dead end, but the field of scientists that are looking at this phenomenon as a purely materialistic function are blind to the current reality involving the communication of electromagnetism between the earth and its inhabitants. It is quite obvious that in the last century of human evolution, there has been a tremendous increase in information spread to all corners of the globe, but this information hasn't been most accurate but rather the opposite. The result of spreading misinformation which is a term that now has general arbitrations means that the dynamics of the earth are interconnected with human behavior which has shown as of late that there is unprecedented suffering. This human behavior is not isolated to the specific type of energy known as fossil fuels but rather to how relationships and organizations are governed which is often construed to a hierarchy of power that leaves the majority exploited.

Further knowledge of the earth being tilted on an axis is the result of an imbalance between the magnetic poles of the earth that tether the collective frequencies in which human beings emit from their choices and current worldview. The tilt of the axis is not a purely natural phenomenon amongst other planets and in some fashion can tilt further depending on whether humanity continues to exacerbate conflict and division leading to a pole shift within the earth. Though possible but unlikely due to certain progressive trends and ideas already spread abroad, it is likely that the condition of climate change will be seen as an issue of ideological fanaticism very much influenced by narcissistic strategies to obtain power and prestige. In the current course of social dynamics, weather will continue to increase in abnormality along with extreme temperature shifts between summer and winter.

It is true that ice caps of the north and south will melt causing rising sea levels that will demand governments to galvanize important resources stored in cities and rebuild important infrastructure inland, but this will not happen all of sudden like the movies or doomsday critics suggest. More animal species will go extinct as well as new evolutions of animals will take place due to mechanisms to adapt to new conditions as well as energies circulating the collective worldview. New forms of technology will be created that follow the innovations of Nikola Tesla as modern pioneers are reinventing his work to allow fossil fuels and even green renewable energies to become obsolete. The environment will be an aspect of life much more of interest to integrate into homes, towns, and cities as a necessity for human wellness because without its reverence we will continue to see the fallout of sociological foundations for human life.

Homelessness

This condition is a direct byproduct of human inaction upon intersectional identification with one another, the inaction to shift out of the current worldview that everyone and everything is a composite of separate objects with separate goals often tinged with competitive ambitions of independent survival. This condition is the most explicit and extreme objective manifestation of humanity's ignorance towards who they are and what capabilities they have. With the aid of historical narcissism or elitism, profound ideologies have been built to justify and convince the majority that homeless is a result of individual choice and effect of choice. There is truth within every lie and so at the soul level the narcissists aren' t wrong but when coupled with the outright strategy to manipulate their capability of discernment by doing a number of things to enrich the elite by devaluing the worth of souls, there is much more to just individual choice.

Not all homeless people are novice souls with minimal experience and knowledge of how the world works as some are advanced souls who either at the result of unfortunate circumstances or by giving up on life which in reality both are unanimously synonymous. Some might say there are too many factors to say whether homelessness is caused by one thing or another and they aren't necessarily wrong, but when you add up certain trends it can be seen that there are really just three basic scenarios at play. One of which I mentioned about intentional strategic narcissistic influence, second is the level of the soul, and the third comprises in one's ability to trust themselves in sharing their deepest love or vision. Now homelessness can be a major change in social identity which can severely test the principles in which one chooses to believe in oneself but there are some out there who do believe in themselves and are what they would call free from anxiety and stress despite the judgment from others.

Society or the government materially can definitely help many of the homeless people have a decent standard of living and many of which would actually get helped but a certain portion would continue to fall not because of drugs but because the collective worldview has not voted in on certain reliable sources of information to how we can treat a soul with trauma not a human being that just has biological compounds that have no objective relevance to a higher identity. Until a critical percentage of national populations can reach a consensus on how we can evaluate "pseudo scientific" data that stems from an immaterial compound of energy largely influencing the everyday choices of people, we will not recognize that these homeless people have perhaps been involved in very traumatic events in previous lifetimes which oftentimes are incited through war.

There is much to unpack about who an individual really is and how to evaluate different psychological wavelengths that synchronize with various unseen geometries or matrices for how society processes itself, we will not be able to significantly treat the soul of anybody especially homeless people. The homeless crisis will get worse especially in cities over time and will reach a peak along with other social malfunctions to budge the academic establishment into a whole new approach to evaluating reliable knowledge based on consciousness and then implementing it. New movements requiring organization to hold non-violent demonstrations will arise to further accelerate the end of homelessness through social welfare and programs, but also give paramount credence to a new worldview involving the meta-world of unseen phenomena.

Women

As said in the LGTBQ+ section, gender is an illusion that may very well have a biological history ascribed to traits found in nature, but the understanding of nature today is still quite skewed from the knowledge we will have one this century ends. It is quite obvious that for a long time women have been chosen to be not only a label in themselves but an inferior label. It is true that we find that men are generally more strong but to the degree in which women cannot do the same tasks as men has been refuted. It is also true that women don't prefer the intellectual hardline tasks as well as physical labor but this can be argued because of social engineering, a process of training individuals to see the world in a specific way to control the general personal identity.

For a long time women have undergone a certain pressure from religion or historical faiths that have been said to be spoken by god but this most certainly can't be true if the results have psychologically denigrated women to a limited social status which is what happened in the distant past and has largely loosened up today. But the trends of history are still enacted today with various types of camouflage but the most obvious reveals how in most businesses especially the monopolies and government have an overwhelming percentage of men running the show. This is a very direct example how the collective worldview still incorporates a type of inferiority towards women especially in the middle east and isolationist countries like russia, china, and to a degree india.

The treatment of women in the more isolationist countries is still quite inhumane and really is a crime that demands grassroot organization and demonstration to restore the essential rights that women deserve. But it should be noted that much of this continues because of the collective belief in gender roles, in this idea that men are men and women are women because that's the way it's always been, which is actually not how it's always been. But through this role the person that acclaims women to their role takes on a huge amount of pressure to a standard of beauty that is deliberately created to bring down self-esteem and create a world of justifiable competition that has a rough process in order to gain notoriety from. This also affects those who take on the male role in a negative way, but the added conscription for women to maintain loyalty or in some cases are pressured to marry and have children at an early age has a large detriment to the gifts they really want to give. Some of these marriages are forced or arranged and if the women were to exist she would be significantly punished which is another humanitarian crime that deserves organized decent.

Women still have quite a bit of progress to achieve but the women's liberation movement is under way and magnificent changes will be happening in these next decades. As with all these topics, much of the change waiting to happen is a result in the acknowledgement of consciousness and the soul, parts of the individual that have been widely denied and ignored due to its remarkable potential to end suffering, conflict, and exploitation. There is much to look forward to as humanity transcends the gender roles that are so often to blame for the abuse, neglect, and infighting that takes place between people and when women begin to speak out especially in the realm of the economy and their essential rights will things really shift.

Drugs

The most widespread use of drugs and alcohol is because people are lonely even with a partner or friends. I'm not saying that drugs specifically have a negative effect but most often they are used to numb the fear that people have towards observing the conscience. I will say that it's often not an easy thing to observe yourself and express your creativity to help remove a portion of suffering that exists in the world because the engineering process is really well done. But as people are given the knowledge, tools, and rehabilitation zones necessary to somewhat decompress and harmonize themselves back into balance, drugs and alcohol won't be seen as the direct solution. It can also be said that the people who have some knowledge of who they are though often they would say they are spiritual or know themselves well, also do concede to the use of drugs and alcohol often as a means to numb because as said before, there is more illusion operating through the progressive movements.

I will say that the use of drugs and alcohol are not bad, sinful, or inherently wrong things to do and that you cannot grow from the use of these things, but there is a very narrow line in how one can use these things without believing in the lie that certain external sources can always give you more interconnection with your true self than your own conscience. The same goes for books, teachers, podcasts, and or whatever content is out there but surely you can grow from continued use of these mediums, but when it comes to drugs and alcohol and yes i'm including weed and psychedelics here, there are often more subtle factors interplaying with one's conscience than is realized because most people who partake in such are not familiar with the mysteries. There are surges right now helping people discover how the universe and consciousness actually work through unified physics, but this arena doesn't have all the answers and quite frankly there is no ultimate answer or source with all answers, but there are consecutive sources throughout time that have given very accurate answers repeatedly without intended or unintended manipulation for deceit.

The mysteries cannot be explained entirely in words but as explained elsewhere, it is a process or path in which one observes their conscience as with the world phenomena and experiments with current knowledge at hand to find more knowledge that interconnects with the mechanism to go beyond current worldviews and identifications. What we find often through the so-called more enlightened portion of psychedelic and weed users is a repeating denial to believe in a force inside one's conscience in order to achieve the next level of being or growth. Oftentimes there is a subconscious mechanism pressuring these people to want an extreme high or rather different way at looking at life though often these ambitions don' t inspire goals to democratically reform certain areas of society let alone their subconscious through educating oneself which is not necessarily done through academia.

I' m not really in favor of punishing people for the use of drugs and certainly I' m not in favor of coercing children and teens through the use of drugs in order to gain a better life experience let alone dumb them down. I know there are cartels, gangs, and underground organizations that have built a whole industry that is tied to those in high positions of power, but do sense as with many of the other topics, that as people know more about themselves and how the world works, how the elite works, more diplomatic enlightened conversations can take place to help humanity see that drug or alcohol usage doesn' t have to be an epic necessity.

Free Will

Not exactly the easiest subject to convey partly because it's one that can never be completely defined through material terminology, but this can surprisingly go for any subject as everything is in a constant state of flux or change. As philosophers, theologians, and scientists have been arguing for quite some time whether free will actually exists and how free is free will, we will try to step back from an overly analytical approach somehow someway ha! So we will start with the basic idea that people have the potential to perceive the most horrendous to the most humanitarian choice of action in response to being given consciousness. There is no doubt that all things are endowed with intelligence as everything is existing within a field of energy constantly vibrating no matter how fast or slow, which would lead us to question how certain mindsets might be able to change the speed at which objects vibrate. But why?

All emotions, thoughts, and personalities are likewise akin to a specific type of vibrating energy often qualified through sound, color, and speed. When applied intention is given to a mode of choice, some form in the material world is bound to be affected differently by means of a specific change of vibration. As some of those reading these words have already presumed that I'm falling on my promise not to analyze this topic, it must be said that there is a type of analysis that camouflages as a means to paralyze and other forms that seek to catalyze universal theory. The topic of free will is theory and will never be proven and can' t be proven so long as a mechanical method is applied to the process of investigation whereby the terms or rules set by those before us are ascribed to a holy ritual that when mistaken deems blasphemy from the surrounding overseers of academia.

Free will in simple terms suggests a certain freedom to change the material world for better or for worse, but the question is who is deciding what is better or worse when this exact difference has been used to justify intellectual inequality to thereby centralize a certain type of individual to be seen as smarter than the majority. It is true we can talk about who gave us free will and by what boundaries are we allowed this freedom of choice given that we cannot consciously manifest certain desires to travel to other planets for example. But most people know this is an entirely unrealistic desire due to the instant split of knowledge to how an individual can practically survive on one of these bodies, so then what is it we really want if we truly have free will?

Many people have different desires but are there unanimous trends, are there patterns that can be traced? Well from the surface it is obvious people want to live more than they want to kill themselves so thereby the work, but people have a very skewed definition of what living means as for many its surviving and numbing. This isn't surprising, but perhaps it can get more obvious by considering a mechanism inside of free will or even consciousness that archetypes a context for how growth can be achieved, growth in awareness. This mechanism can be likened to allowing an individual to perceive that they themselves have the sovereign power to remove the ability to choose for another person. Having this freedom in place allows for a mixture of almost infinite possibilities of existing diversity to manifest themselves whereby people can choose and evaluate whether unconditional love or egocentric control is what they wish to believe is real. But will people go beyond their reality they have built if they tire of suffering, survival, and competition is a question answered only as a newfound inspiration to be more.

Conspiracies

The idea that someone can be against you is ancient and the idea of pain is also ancient but do these two forms of human experience really exist? If the universal mechanism built into the fabric of choice gives back to the individual agent what they conceive through choice multiplied, what wrong in conspiring evil can coexist through a recycling universe? I understand how this question can be difficult to contend with when you add the age old story of narcissists coming up with numerous schemes to out-compete what I will refer to as the novice souls or original inhabitants. There is a lot I cannot say here but it is difficult to understand how energy can be recycled given there have been countless epochs where the free will simulator that we call earth has been clogged, has been charged with countless tragedies and deaths. But one thing people don' t realize is another plot out there to use all the qualified energy known as suffering as a deterrent to avenge the fallen and reconcile civilization back into harmony.

Though there are good intentions involved with this plot, most people involved actually in fact all individuals involved don' t understand einstein's quote on consciousness but neither don' t they understand the onion layer of progressive revelation.

The word revelation has a tidal wave of facetious corroborated compounds indicated by the religious movements to suggest in academia that it is a syndrome of incoherent pretexts that begets no plausible investigation. But the anger of science often at the bestowal of countless traumatic events of persecution has swung the pendulum to the opposite extreme to thereby deny the allowance of true progressive revelation by labeling it a common quirk of religious outcry when the very nature of what I speak has very little to do with worldwide faiths.

There has already been some scientific investigation into this subject mentioned above, but the nature of its specification deals with the control panel for how free will is shaped and patterns throughout the world. There is much on this subject I cannot complete here, but the control panel that has been foretold by some unified physicists but also by those outside of this field suggests that when you try to control, blame, or label anybody as evil, a conspirator, a dark member of a cabal that is trying to enslave the population through psycho-strategic blueprints, you begin to concoct your own frankenstein's monster. There is truth in every lie as there have been many elites that have sought power, control, and explicit outright suffering through many timelines, but there is another form of vindictive power struggle that currently is humanity's

last "enemy" even though we are really just talking
about ideas rather than persons here.

As you can see I have written three
paragraphs without specifically stating one specific
conspiracy whether that be JFK's assasination or
9/11 and now the big one is vaccines even though
there are over a hundred conspiracies out there that
suggest serious attention is needed to resolve the
conflict at hand. Horrible things have happened but
how horrible are they really when you follow the
energetic bread crumbs of energy identifications?
When you continue to see how free will expresses
itself and how it can be manipulated to the nth
degree, a person will organically awaken to the
nature of universal principles being the axiomatic
leverage tool to accelerate consciousness or rather
bring light to ignored facets of human choice, human
interest. These principles require courage and a
sense of determination sometimes to push through,
but eventually those who consider themselves
enlightened will be easily recognized from those who
are inflaming the plot line to thereby vilify a few
and victimize the many.

Sex

The phenomenon of sex is quite unique when you take in all the things people do to survive and all the judgement and suffering in the world you have this thing called sex, a thing whereby two people can find an extraordinary sense of union. But this doesn' t happen so often anymore despite the industry of sex skyrocketing proportionally and this is because the phenomenon is more often used to extract an external euphoria versus an internal connection with the person. There is nothing inherently wrong with this, it just so happens that when the soul is deflected from one of the most exhilarating experiences found on earth, a feedback system is then created to deflect the individual soul choosing to participate. And whenever this is deflection there is a type of entropy that will vary depending on how intensely the individual is just trying to have a good time without wanting to know more of the person they are connecting with.

This entropy can take on many forms and it may not even be so intense if the person isn' t so involved in the industry but chances are when they are, a snowball effect will take position unless that individual has trained to observe their own conscience without reacting. This snowball effect influences a significant amount of people all over the world, especially the youth. We are at a time where kids are not given a proper perspective of how the world works and what we are really capable of beyond being some doctor, lawyer, engineer, or scientist. When this happens while simultaneously allowing the industries of sex to comingle into the entertainment industry, an industry that has always been deeply connected with the youth, a collective beast begins to form. For the last 50 years, an unprecedented degree of strategized hyperfixation on specific parts of the body through the industry has led to a rewiring effect in the collective mainframe.

Everything I'm saying should be obvious but proceeding along this line, the basic result of the beast is to minimize energy or rather the thoughts and ideas taking place between people to cooperate and evolve. Never before has there been such a sexualization of conversation between people, especially on the side of men to further denigrate the inherent creativity that has almost infinite ways of suggesting a bright world, a better world based on cooperation. The entertainment industry has such a blind understanding of what love is that it's constantly projecting a radioactive force of culture which I named a type of beast, that really has only one interest which is to erode the rights of people. But I will sympathize and say the other purpose for this scenario is to show people the basic effect of

what happens when we play into these social
identifications.

But it should be mentioned as said before,
that long long ago, even before known records of
intelligent civilization, a certain choice was made to
separate not just people into male and female
identifications but a choice was made to separate
energies of masculine and feminine. This has led to a
huge rift between people because our natural state is
a unique balance between these qualities. I can talk
more about how these qualities don't actually mean
what society thinks they mean, but trends are on the
verge of breaking the mold for what we know love
really means. We aren't there yet and things are
going to get a bit more extreme within the era of
cyber technology and cyberpunk culture to lead to the
creation of cybersex with robots, but the long term
future does take a positive turn whereby sex isn't
so defining anymore.

Terrorism

As stated before, the greatest terror on earth
is that death is real but for certain portions of the
world there is somewhat of a bigger terror that feeds
on this fear of death and uses the tactic of
fundamentalist fanaticism, a tactic that has been
used by many religions but most especially islam with
the term jihad. The root meaning of jihad is actually
positive, but down the line of history it was hijacked
and then people believed that unless they obeyed the
scripture of a religion, it should be carried out in
god's name that people take it upon themselves to
eliminate others even if that means sacrificing one's
self. This has created a weird interference pattern in
the collective worldview that piggybacks on top of
many other worldviews that we as people should fear
death but more especially the punishment of dying if
it comes through the authority of god. In previous
ages there would be raids on villages, cities and even
wars in the name of god because a group didn't
believe in correct beliefs about god which has helped
create modern day terrorism in a unique way.

Through the rise of democracy and a more
democratic state of affairs in the world, the utter
use to create a war to conquer or punish others will
be seen as insane to most people. But with more
advanced technology enabling people to kill each

other much quicker, a certain force has taken upon itself to continue the age-old directive to ensure god's law or kingdom remains pure. Through the use of suicide bombings and or militant warlords using governments, there has been a continued pressure to ensure the right way of life is enforced at all costs despite the amount of peace achieved in the world. Even though modern democracies are relatively peaceful areas, there are still many forms of knowledge that people don' t understand and as stated in the beginning, the knowledge of death as an illusion is the biggest one. So then this triggers a big reaction in people if all of a sudden there is a bombing or an attack on a nation-state that is widely peaceful.

Oftentimes as narcissists like to be in control, especially in government positions where they can have the most control, the financial elite see quite well how certain situations like this can feed the war machine, the belief beast of suggesting killing others is not only justifiable but it is most certainly profitable. And so throughout the ages war has been seen as an honorable culture, a form of entertainment where certain individuals can gain notoriety and others can enjoy the spectacle. To this very day we still have industries that are similar to those of old whereby the movies and games we play often have significant ties to killing which subconsciously proliferate consent into the minds of everyday citizens to real life killing. This is a big reason the war in iraq was able to be accepted by the majority of americans but also curtailing on this fear of death and by any means necessary should we use force to prevent death from happening again.

Naturally we are still in a time period of climatic spikes where war is still seen as somewhat necessary and honorable especially with men around the world. But we are moving faster through technological capacities enabling people to form their own opinion about war than what is suggested by government patterns of old. The forseeable future shows that war is on its last legs and will be soon coming to an end on earth despite the continued acts of terrorism or empirical tyranny that some of the more isolated countries to continue to show today. The fear of death is progressively becoming less of a concern and so then will terrorism.

Entertainment

Ah the resplendent culture of comfort, humor, and ecstatic wonder, what an interesting phenomenon. Through the onset of orwell's 1984 novel, huxley's brave new world, le guin's omelas, the matrix, and squid game as mainstream perspectives into the world of social engineering, the public has a really weird contention going on in their minds when they dip their souls in modern entertainment. There is a dual personality effect that is more noticeable within certain people than others, but the unilateral progression of depression is seeping into the collective norm, the way things just are. There is a very specific code interwoven into many of the entertainment models used around the world, especially modern democratic nations whereby the business line for profit is highly of interest and this line has a direct effect on democracy, education, and even the level of acceptance a human being has for oneself.

It has been said that entertainment is the steering wheel of civilization and that all advancements and reliable forms of knowledge come through the advent of cultural games and interactives with one another. This is why it's important the entertainment industry is regulated by universal principles and wisdom so that we don't find ourselves at a point where we end up creating a real world tragedy causing people to be passive or extremists. The current trend in the world naturally creates an effect of division amongst the people and unity amongst the most ruthless members of society, those scourging for more and more profit. The question is how do we detect these universal principles if for so much of history these examples are so hidden? By looking at specific trends, perhaps radical trends, that have shown a mixture of comedy, romance, and conflict in ways that aren' t so normal.

To describe these abnormal ways is really quite difficult to portray but certain individuals have shown there are ways to re-educate the masses without making them feel they' re being educated. The modern form of education and studying is really just a lazy way of figuring out how a life works when in fact another form co-exists that doesn' t really require any paperwork or compensation that can really show how all human beings have more in common than we realize. But it' s so hard to talk about when our culture is steeped in glorifying violence, sexualizing the soul, and polarizing the elite in vindictive ways that insinuate anger that overtime incites unrest. Violence, sex, and comedy politics is not wrong or bad in itself, its just something that can very much create major energetic chaos if it' s effects are not investigated and discussed.

Modern entertainment has a windy road ahead of us but will ultimately find its course of balance. As artificial intelligence and virtual realities become more accessible, especially to the youth, there will be many glitches in the system of human identification whereby depression, suicide, and abuse will surge even more due to the toxicity of modern culture continue extremifying itself. Animation technology is an area that is becoming more accessible to anyone and without a critical challenge to the normative qualities of modern entertainment, humanity will continue to experience newfound horror stories in the VR world but in general entertainment usage as well. Humanity will eventually get over our veiled idolatry to the world of extremes but until then entertainment will continue to spike various types of suffering and with the use of robots it will become more apparent to what perceptions could actually be harming our rights to treat everyone with respect and dignity, most especially ourself.

History

There are many ideas that many experts would want me to back up, especially from an ontological perspective that may have some credibility but due to the ignorance we have towards history, there are many points that can' t be proven. It is true that there are many experts who have traced the dustbins of history to the center of public opinion to thus accredit their labor and knowledge with a degree that may pay them well. But history cannot truly be told, studied, or researched if we don' t have the other side of the coin, the side that was burnt, killed, or interpolated that very well could have shown an alternative reality more plausible. Between the lines of the ideas shared through this compilation there are small suggestions about the events of history being different than what is told to us in the textbooks. My self ascribed credentials will be the laughing stock for further balk and rebuke towards the previous statements I have made about history as many requests for evidence will be the target of measuring my merit.

I' m not really going to say anything about specific events in history for there is nothing I can really say due to the large quantification of information being erased whether through myth, story, or literature, I know there is information today about a world of records that goes beyond what we have today. I will remain an academic fool in the eyes of so many who do not wish to consider alternative sources for obtaining objective accounts of the true events of history. The objective sources can be tested and proven over time repeatedly and have been investigated but with largely biased regards to give biased results. Science is still very angry with religion and is largely winning the so-called war of the wise though in reality nobody wins in war despite what the historians say. For the victors will often purport the ideas least tolerable in the eyes of compassion and wisdom and this can be marked through the two different authors of similar name; sun-tzu and lao-tzu, both signifying a very different reality for how life success is obtained.

So as the world continues to contend with critics, analysts, debate lords, and various ideologues for who has the most objective truth to be recognized as the savior of reliable knowledge, more people will deal with plain old depression because life doesn' t work through the mind only. The mind is a tool that when tempered with the heart or rather the human who doesn' t care for such analytical procedures or intellectual systems for obtaining knowledge, a foundation of credible long-lasting information can be used to build common ground. But right now in the subject of history, there is very little common ground because we can' t even recognize the tactics of elitism and aristocracy. If we did truly recognize them we would see the handwriting on the wall and express our soulful creativity through different mediums beyond pure intellectual battles. Social media is a bit of a mess right now and it will get messier. The academic colosseum continues to threaten the public with fear of survival lest a degree is obtained, lest one obeys to the ivory towers of rhetoric and dialectics that has no place in the heart of consciousness evolution.

Democracy, civilization, and the human identity is being reborn and there will be continued battles to prove to one another that a forbidden history is being revealed, a history of secrecy and taboo that spells out all the manipulations the elites have used to get people to believe they were never smart enough to have a society based on love and wisdom. But through the annals of time history will become less relevant with pure human imagination.